#Justice For Ashley

A Shocking True Crime Story

Rod Kackley

Published by Rod Kackley, 2019.

#JUSTICE FOR ASHLEY

First edition. November 19, 2019.

Written by Rod Kackley.

"You, sir, in my mind, are a very evil individual. You are clearly a monster without any conscience whatsoever,"

Kent County Judge Mark Trusock

"God gave me the gift of Ashley. You had no right to take her from me!"

Kristine Young

Chapter One

"You don't deserve to breathe," yells a woman as she holds a container filled with her daughter's ashes. The object of her outrage; the man convicted of killing her adult child, a thirty-one-year-old woman who had everything to live for until one fateful night eleven months ago.

However, the enraged woman isn't finished. The sentencing of her daughter's murderer is the woman's last chance to vent, and she isn't about to mince words. It doesn't matter that she is in a court of law, standing before a judge. This is still her moment. The woman is looking right at the man who'd murdered her baby girl, and she isn't about to let him off easy.

In Michigan, this is when crime victims and their survivors are allowed to let loose on the person convicted of doing them harm and hopefully convince the judge in the case to forget any thought of leniency.

The killer, knowing he'll probably spend the rest of his life behind bars, is silent. He doesn't move or even blink. If there's any emotion in him at all, it's hidden away, below the surface. His heart couldn't be farther from his sleeve.

"You threw her out like trash," the woman screams, not loosening her grip on the urn, knowing she'd never again be able to touch her child.

Adding to the injury of the insult of losing a child to a homicidal maniac is the knowledge that the killer refuses to tell anyone where he hid his victim's head, hands, and feet.

That's right. Not only had he killed, but this animal of a human being had also sawed her daughter's body to pieces, leaving the torso beneath a bloody tarp and other parts of her body in a cardboard box.

But the head, feet, and hands of the victim, have yet to be found. And they won't if the murderer has anything to say about it. The killer—a slight, scrawny, redhead— vows to never give his victim's survivors the satisfaction, the closure, of being able to lay the dead woman, completely, to rest.

"You will never tell me where she is because you like to torment people, you like to hurt them, you enjoy it," the woman yells at the top of her lungs. "I hate you. I want to rip you limb from limb and discard you like trash."

She's not alone.

The victim's father is also in the courtroom. "May you rot in hell," he tells his daughter's convicted killer. "You lived your life as a coward — you will die as a coward."

"You are the devil," the victim's stepmother sobs. "Even the death penalty is too good for you."

The victim's grandmother also takes a turn to speak as the killer stands emotionless, staring straight ahead, quietly listening to the rage of those whose lives he'd ruined, soaking it all in.

"Your eyes are empty," she says. "Where is your soul?"

Chapter Two

There is a chill in the air, as Ashley Young, an attractive, dark-haired, thirty-one-year-old woman, arrives at Mulligan's Pub in the trendy southeast side neighborhood, Eastown, in Grand Rapids, Michigan.

Just three days ago, daytime temperatures were in the low forties and overnight lows in the upper thirties. That's balmy for late November in western Michigan. But this night, temperatures were locked in the high twenties during the day and stayed consistent throughout the night. So, Ashley is glad to get out of the bitter winter chill as she opens the door to Mulligan's and joins the happy, laughing, and above all, warm crowd out for a night of celebration.

Thanksgiving was a week ago, beginning the winter holiday season. Plenty of students in Grand Rapids — which is as much a college town as it is anything else — have the week off, and lots of them show up in taverns like Mulligan's to meet with old friends.

Grand Rapids city officials had worked for several years to make their city, which for decades had a reputation as a cold, forbidding, overly religious community, into a place that welcomes thee twenty-first-century and the generation that came along with it. That's why the city embraced its new nickname, "Beer City USA." It worked. The Eastown bar scene attracted scores of millennials like Ashley, who were just beginning their adult lives.

Now, it's close to midnight. Mulligan's is packed. Typical for the pub. Just as there's nothing unusual about the weather outside, bartender Emily Potgetter doesn't notice anything strange about Ashley and the twenty-nine-year-old man she is with, a skinny red-haired guy with a mustache and light beard, Jared Chance.

Neither of them is from Grand Rapids, but both are native to western Michigan. Ashley calls the Kalamazoo-area community of Oshtemo Township home. Jared was born and raised near Holland, Michigan.

Ashley and Jared had a relationship a few years ago. But her mother warned her to stay away from him, especially after he broke into her apartment and stole a few things. Jared was nothing but trouble as far as Kristine Young, Ashley's mom, was concerned.

However, one of her friends convinced Ashley to get back together with Jared on Facebook. One message led to another, and wouldn't you know it, here they are, Ashley and Jared back together again.

Jared is drinking Budweiser tonight, while Ashley orders a couple of Patron tequilas. She doesn't finish her drinks. No matter. Ashley's happy. She and Jared are becoming close again, cuddly close.

Jared and Ashley's night doesn't end at Mulligan's. They leave early the next morning. Bars close at two a.m. in Michigan. The crowd streams out of the warmth of Mulligan's Pub into the chill of Eastown. Lots of people will look for a 24-hour diner, like Wolfgang's here in Eastown, or Grand Coney on the city's northeast side, for an early-morning breakfast. But not Ashley and Jared.

The couple stays together and walks into Miss Tracy's Liquor Store a couple hours after leaving Mulligan's. Miss Tracy's is far removed from Mulligan's Pub and the Eastown neighborhood, both geographically and culturally. One Yelp review called the store "ghetto."

If Miss Tracy's isn't part of Grand Rapids millennial generation renaissance, neither is Jared's home. He lives in a brown, two-story World War Two-era wood-frame duplex house, about a block from Miss Tracy's where he rents an apartment.

Fast forward a few hours, and Jared is back at Miss Tracy's. This time he's sans Ashley and, on the way in, tosses several items into the trash bin outside the store. Jared goes inside the store, grabs some beer out of the cooler, takes it to the front, and pays for the six-pack with a credit card. But beer isn't all Jared wants, he's done a little bit more shopping.

After finishing his credit card transaction for the beer, Jared puts a container of ammonia on the counter. He pays for that with cash.

Chapter Three

Nov. 29, 2018

Ashley's mother, Kristine Young, is frantic. She knows something is wrong. Kristine keeps getting Ashley's voice mail when she calls. Yet, her panic is fueled by more than an inability to reach her daughter. Kristine's reached out to Ashley's friends and other family members. Nobody has heard from the 31-year-old woman who Kristine describes as "kind, loving, and infectious."

Kristine knows this is serious. She feels it.

Finally, she calls Jared Chance. Kristine doesn't like it, but she knows he and her daughter are close. This is her last resort. If Jared hasn't seen her, Kristine doesn't know what she'll do.

Jared tells Kristine that he and Ashley had gone to Mulligan's Pub the night before. After that, Jared says, Ashley went to Kalamazoo. He's talked and texted with her since then, Jared says. Everything's alright; he assures Kristine.

Jared even gives her names and phone numbers of several people who, he says, Ashley was planning to see in Kalamazoo. So, Kristine calls and texts each and every one of them. Every single message turns up a goose egg. One guy, who Jared claimed Ashley was planning to see in Kalamazoo, tells Kristine he's never heard of Ashley and has absolutely no idea who she could be.

Taking her search to a whole new level, proving she's a mother who can't be stopped, Kristine gets in touch with the people who run Mulligan's and demands to see the surveillance video from Nov. 28. She wants to make sure Jared's at least telling her the truth about taking Ashley to the bar.

And, sure enough, there she is. Kristine sees Ashley on the Mulligan's videotape. Talk about bittersweet. Kristine's heart is broken. There she is. Ashley, live and well. Kristine wants to reach into the computer monitor and pull her daughter off the screen.

Of course, she can't. Reality sets in. Ashley is missing, and no one seems to know where she might be.

It's time, Kristine decides to stop doing this on her own. Since Jared said Ashley was going to Kalamazoo, she files a missing-person report with that city's police department.

While she is doing that, Jared is asking one of his neighbors to help him move a car from their shared driveway. Later, the neighbor would remember it was the vehicle he saw Jared and "a white girl" get out of a day ago. The neighbor watched both walk into their house. But, later, he would remember never seeing the woman leave.

Chapter Four

Dec. 1, 2018

Jared's parents, James and Barbara, along with his younger brother Konrad, pile into their Honda and drive north on I-196 into Grand Rapids, today, to pick up Jared.

Barbara's driving. It is a mild day for December in western Michigan. Temperatures have rebounded from the bitter cold of a few days ago. And, here is a bonus — no snow. But it is cloudy again. The sun hadn't broken through for more than a month. This is another gloomy day, which doesn't help the mood in the Chance vehicle.

Everybody in the car is tense — on edge.

But, still, thanks to the dry pavement, it should be an easy drive for the parents and their son from Holland, northeast along the Lake Michigan shoreline, into Grand Rapids.

When the family arrives at Jared's apartment, after navigating through the narrow, often one-way streets of Grand Rapids, the 2007 Holland High School graduate gets into the Honda, bringing along a cardboard box. Inside is something; nobody can see just what, wrapped in a black, plastic garbage bag. Even with that protection, though, the bottom of the box is soggy and leaking. Still, Jared tosses it into the Honda.

The family drives Jared to their home in Holland, less than an hour away from Grand Rapids. However, before they leave the southeast side of Grand Rapids, they pull up alongside

Jared's car, which he'd parked a few streets away from his duplex apartment.

Jared hops out the Honda, dashes through the cold to his car, and takes a box out of the trunk. He runs back to his family's car and places it alongside the other cardboard container in the Honda.

With the new cargo on board, the family continues its trip southwest along I-196 to their home in Holland, a community with a well-deserved reputation for lockstep Christianity and conservative Republican politics.

While the Chance family is taking Jared and his mysterious cargo to their home in Holland, from Grand Rapids, Kristine Young is in her car, too. She's driving north on U.S. 131 into Grand Rapids.

She gets off at the downtown Grand Rapids exit and drives a few blocks to Grand Rapids Police Department Headquarters at 1 Monroe Center, in the heart of the city's downtown district.

Inside, Kristine has a conversation with GRPD Lt. Patrick Merrill. Kristine tells Lt. Merrill, a white-haired cop who wears black-framed glasses, all about her daughter.

She tells him more than he needs to know, but Merrill's been around. He knows a worried parent when he sees one. And the lieutenant senses the woman's correct. Her daughter is in danger.

Kristine also tells Lt. Merrill his department ought to be looking at Jared Chance. Merrill takes her advice. A GRPD officer is sent to talk to Jared at his house on the southeast side of the city. But nobody's home. Jared's on his way to Holland with his parents and brother. So that's a conversation that will have to wait for another day.

Chapter Five

Dec. 2, 2018

Lt. Merrill's back at work inside the Grand Rapids Police Department's headquarters building when he hears a couple of interns at the front desk in a heated conversation with a man who's complaining about people harassing his son on Facebook.

Lt. Merrill sighs and gets back to his work until he hears the name Jared Chance mentioned by the angry man. Bingo! Lt. Merrill steps out of his office to find out who's talking about Jared and encounters none other than Jared and his father, James Chance.

Sometimes it's better to be lucky than good, right? Lt. Merrill's not about to miss this opportunity. He asks Jared if Ashley was with him a few days ago and if he's seen her since then.

Jared confirms he and Ashley went to Mulligan's but insists he hasn't seen her since Nov. 30. That day, Jared says, Ashley told him she had to be at work by six o'clock, so she left his house. Not what he told Kristine, is it?

If Lt. Merrill thought James Chance was angry when he complained to the GRPD interns about Jared being harassed on Facebook, he hadn't seen anything yet.

James becomes even angrier at Lt. Merrill's questioning of Jared and demands he stop. Lt. Merrill asks one more question about Ashley. James, again, demands, there be no more questions.

But Lt. Merrill asks an additional question.

"What's your address?" Lt. Merrill says to Jared.

James and Jared turn their backs on the officer and walk out of GRPD Headquarters onto Monroe Center.

The entire exchange takes less than a minute. Back at the car Jared decides to grab his soggy cardboard box with the black plastic garbage bag inside and go back to the southeast side duplex he calls home.

Chapter Six

Something smells. Bad. Mario Nelson, a young black man who lives in the duplex unit below Jared, decides to investigate. Actually, it is Mario's girlfriend, Yashieka Christian, who decides he should go downstairs and investigate. So, Mario finds himself walking down the stairs into the basement.

Mario might not want to admit it, but his girl was right. Something is really wrong done here. The smell is getting worse. Most worrisome, this isn't the kind of odor generated by a sewer pipe backing up, or a bag of garbage left to rot. Mario knows this is something much worse. Something died down here, he's sure of it.

Going down the stairs is the easy part of his investigative journey. Once Mario's on the ground floor, it's tough getting into the basement. Their landlord doesn't allow either Jared or Mario access to the basement. But both tenants had figured out how to squeeze past the washer and dryer that are installed in a common area to get into the basement. So, Mario presses forward.

Once past the washer and dryer, Mario follows the smell as if he was playing the game he played as a kid where Mario was said to be getting warmer as he got closer to the object, person, or goal of his search. Mario was told he was getting colder if he went the wrong way.

Well, judging by the rank odor that fills the basement, Mario is getting warmer. Finally, Mario is hot. Red hot. He finds a tarp. Mario can't tell what it is covering. Well, Mario suspects he knows what is under the tarp, but he doesn't want to be the one to pull it back. There is a small stream of thick, brownish-red blood on the basement floor. It leads to the tarp. What else could it be, except what Mario fears?

If he is correct about what is under the tarp, Mario thinks he has a pretty good idea of who is responsible.

Jared.

Mario had always had his doubts about the guy. Once, while they were smoking pot and getting high together in Jared's apartment, Marlo was shocked when Jared pulled out a .22-caliber gun. Jared, waving the gun around, followed that with a discussion of how to use soda pop to clean up a crime scene. Not clear enough? Jared even bragged he knew how to murder someone and get away with it.

Unbelievably, Jared took the conversation to an even higher level of bullshit, Mario recalled, when he said his father, a retired cop from Illinois, was actually a made-man in the Irish mob.

So, without looking under the tarp for the source of the blood, Mario calls 911.

Mario tells the dispatcher about the bloody tarp he's discovered.

"There's blood in my basement," he says, "I don't know if it's normal for anybody else, but there's not supposed to be blood in my basement.

"I need police to come here ASAP and take a look at it."

It doesn't take long for a GRPD squad car to show up outside the house at 922 Franklin SE. Officers go inside, talk to Mario, and head to the basement. Sure enough, the officers find a stream of blood coming out from under a tarp. Mario hasn't touched the tarp. That's good. Officers gingerly pull it up and discover the secret it's been hiding for who knows how long.

A human torso.

No hands. No head. No feet. Only stumps for legs that had been sawed off just above the knees. Pretty much the same for the arms. Obviously, the cops could tell it was a woman's body, but that's all the uniforms who were the first GRPD officers through the door had to go on. Still, it is enough though to ratchet this investigation to the highest level of police interest.

As a result, the streets leading to the 900-block of Franklin SE are soon filled with police vehicles as they rush to investigate what prompted Mario's 911 call. Talk about a spectacle of flashing red and blue lights.

It's not that the people in this neighborhood had never seen a GRPD squad car. The people who lived in this part of town had seen more than their fair share of crime of the police

But this level of first-responder response was unusual, even in this neighborhood.

The GRPD investigators decide to move from their discovery of the torso to Jared and his apartment.

However, before they get to the two-bedroom, one-bath unit Jared calls home, the officers find a box with a shipping label addressed to Jared.

Inside the cardboard container, officers discover some human body parts that had probably been removed from the torso in the basement. Pieces of arms and legs. Had to come from the torso under the tarp. After all, how many bodies in this neighborhood could be missing their limbs?

While a forensic unit secures the box and the human limbs, detectives continue up the stairs to Jared's apartment.

Inside that unit, detectives find Jared, barefoot, wearing sweatpants and a green short-sleeved t-shirt. The officers also discover traces of what look like blood in the upstairs bathroom and bathtub. They find human tissue in the kitchen sink trap and smears of red blood on the stairwell that goes down to the duplex's main level.

The detectives decide they've also discovered their prime suspect, Jared Chance.

Chapter Seven

The night of Dec. 2, 2018

The sounds of a police dog barking, a glass window breaking, a fist pounding on a door, and the words, "Police open the door! Grand Rapids Police. Come to the door!" reverberate through the 900-block of Franklin Street SE as a GRPD SWAT team storms Jared's home.

"He's on the third floor! Come on down!" the head of the GRPD unit yells when he spots Jared at the top of the staircase. "Hands on top of your head!"

A voice from inside the house tells the police officers, "the tarp is lying on the stairs, the last three stairs."

Of course, that's the bloody tarp that was hiding a human torso sans hands, feet, and head.

"Hands over your head!" the GRPD cop leading the assault shouts when Jared doesn't respond quickly enough.

He knows the drill. Accustomed to being arrested, Jared finally complies and is led outside.

It's a frigid night to be forced out of your house barefoot, wearing a green t-shirt, long white underwear, and nothing else.

Jared is surprisingly calm, or maybe he's just so confused that he's very compliant. But Jared doesn't give the officers any trouble. He's been here before.

"What's your name?" an officer says.

"Jared."

"What's your last name?"

"Chance."

"Jared Chance."

"Yeah."

Jared's clean-shaven this evening, standing barefoot on the cold pavement as officers pat him down to his ankles, searching for weapons.

He's put into the hard, uncomfortable backseat of a GRPD SUV, hands cuffed behind his back, as an officer fastens a seatbelt and shoulder strap for Jared.

Riding to the GRPD's headquarters building downtown, Jared yawns and looks out the passenger side window with his mouth hanging open.

Jared hasn't said a word since the police asked for his name. Surprisingly, Jared hasn't asked anyone why he's been arrested, or if, in fact, he has been arrested.

Calmly, Jared exits the SUV in the basement large of the headquarters building and is lead into an interrogation room.

Officers ask if he'd like his handcuffs removed. Jared, still amazingly calm and relaxed, says he would, thank you. A uniformed officer tells the female detective who removes his cuffs that it's okay if she leaves the white-walled, small windowless room for a minute.

"You guys stay pretty busy, don't you?" Jared asks the cop who stays in the interrogation room.

Jared's elbows are on the table in front of him, his head in his hands, as he waits for two female detectives who will question him.

Finally they arrive.

"You came in earlier, and I'm sorry you got turned away," one of the detectives says, referring to the visit Jared and James made earlier in the day to talk about Ashley's disappearance.

"Yeah," Jared replies, staring at the top of the table in front of him. Then, he explains.

"I just came in to talk because I read on Facebook that the last person (Ashley) was with was me. So, I was just concerned and wanted to get some information."

Now, Jared's starting to look nervous. He's rubbing his hands together in front of him. Then, Jared moves his right hand to his forehead, and says, "'Cause I don't know what the hell is going on, so I don't want to sit here and talk about shit that.."

Jared puts his hands together and sniffs. Now he seems to finally understand what's going on. Jared's voice is starting to break as he finishes the sentence, "...that might incriminate me or whatever.

"I don't know what's going on. I don't want to say nothing right now."

With that, Jared's taken from the interrogation room, searched again, and moved into a holding cell.

It's time to talk to a lawyer.

Chapter Eight

Dec. 5, 2018

While Jared is being officially changed today with mutilating a dead body and concealing the death of an individual in Grand Rapids, Holland Police Department squad cars and a GRPD forensic evidence unit are blocking the 100-block of West 20th Street in Holland. They've already towed away a vehicle that was parked outside the house, the home of James and Barbara Chance, the residence where James was taken a few days before. Now they're going through the house with their proverbial fine-tooth combs, looking for evidence that could help pin a murder on Jared.

Inside the house, the fastidious investigators make a shocking discovery. They reach under a couch in the living room and pull out a bloody Skil reciprocating saw, the kind of tool that could have been used to cut the arms and legs off that torso found under a tarp in Jared's duplex.

Any speculation about what the saw might have been used for vanishes when the forensic investigators make a gruesome discovery. They find drops of dried human blood and pieces of human tissue on the saw.

Now the Chance family is dealing with even more trouble, and undoubtedly, a higher legal bill because James and Barbara will be charged with lying to police and being accessories after the fact to the mutilation charge.

Police believe James and Barbara knew Jared had cut up Ashley's body with that saw and "hid some of the pieces," according to court records. Prosecutors also say James and Barbara were fully aware Ashley was dead because Jared told them she had died, and he had sawed the body to pieces.

If they're convicted of being an accessory after the fact, James and Barbara could be sentenced to a maximum of five years in prison. That's small change compared to the penalty for lying to a cop. Prosecutors are calling that perjury, and conviction could mean life in prison.

Meanwhile, it turns out that one reason Jared might have seemed so comfortable in the back of that GPRD SUV was that he's no stranger to the process of being arrested and booked for a crime.

He was busted by Allegan County officials — Holland is divided by the Allegan-Ottawa county line — in 2015 for possession of cocaine and marijuana, along with an impaired driving charge. Three years before, Jared was arrested for driving while impaired and giving a false statement to police officers.

His first encounter with law enforcement involved a charge of resisting/obstructing a police officer in 2011. That charge was pleaded down to a probation violation.

Jared's record includes several speeding tickets, a car crash where he was cited for failure to stop, multiple charges of possession of alcohol when he was under the age of 21, and his driver's license was suspended because of an Allegan County drug crime.

"It really doesn't surprise me that he (Jared) is being charged with some kind of hurtful crime," one of Jared's Holland High School classmate, Jessica Thielbar, said to a Holland Sentinel reporter. "He was always rough around the edges.

"To know I sat in a lunchroom with him has put a knot in my stomach."

Chapter Nine

Dec. 7, 2018

Kristine Young's worst fears are realized today. At least one question has been settled. As Kristine lies in bed, trying to get some sleep, she now knows the sad truth. The torso found under the tarp in Jared Chance's basement is all that's left of her daughter.

Well, there is a little more of Ashley that's been discovered. Her arms and parts of her legs were left in that cardboard box on the stairs. And, the bits of human tissue and the blood on the saw found in the Holland Township house — that's Ashley, too.

Grand Rapids Police confirmed it all late today with only a brief announcement on Twitter.

"Update of death investigation involving female remains: DNA has positively identified them of the missing 31 yo Kalamazoo County woman, Ashley Young."

Of course, they couldn't use the standard means of identifying Ashley. Since her head and hands are still MIA, there was no way to check dental records or fingerprints.

Instead, the GRPD had to ship everything to the Michigan State Police Crime Lab to test the DNA. The results came back today, a positive match for Ashley Young, who died at the young age of 31.

DNA expert David Hayhurst works in the biology and DNA unit of the MSP's Grand Rapids Forensic Lab. He says the match is about as decisive as positive can get. It is 1.7 septillion times more likely to be Ashley's DNA than that of a random individual.

Hayhurst adds Young's DNA was also found in a large, reddish-brown stain on the tiled kitchen floor in Jared's apartment. More of Ashley's DNA was on a bloody sweatshirt stuffed into the cardboard fan box on the stairs in the duplex. Investigators also found Ashley's DNA in a blood smear on the molding of a closet door in the kitchen, as well as on a saw blade that detectives found on Jared's porch.

In all, more than 250 DNA samples were taken from Jared's home and his parents' house.

But even though the match was 1.7 septillion times more likely to be Ashley's DNA, the MSP GR Forensic Lab couldn't call the evidence "conclusive."

In addition, forensic examiners have been unable to determine the cause of death, and may not be able to reach that conclusion until Ashley's head is recovered.

While Kristine lays her head down at home, grappling with the tragic news that Ashley is gone, Jared will spend another night on a cot in the Kent County jail. He's being held on a $750,000 bond facing charges of failing to report a death and mutilating a body.

No, he hasn't been charged with murder. Prosecutors have a problem stepping up the charges because forensic examiners have not, however, been able to determine the cause of death.

How could there be any doubt. After all, that sweatshirt found in the fan box was Ashley's, and it was splattered with blood. So, it could be that she was beaten to death or shot in the head. But investigators can't tell for sure without more evidence. Specifically, they need more body parts.

There's no way to say this except to be brutally honest. Finding out why and how Ashley died will have to wait until her head and neck recovered.

Yet, Dr. David Start, the medical examiner who performed the autopsy on Ashley's remains says he can be sure that the young woman's death was neither natural nor the result of an overdose.

So, Dr. Start is ruling Ashley's death to be the result of "homicide by unspecified means."

Chapter Ten

Dec. 14, 2018

Kristine Young stands in front of the Chance family home this evening, talking to a WOOD-TV news crew from Grand Rapids. She's speaking to the reporter and the camera, but really, Kristine says her message is for Barbara Chance.

Saying she is speaking mother-to-mother, Kristine pleads for the return of her daughter's head, hands, and feet. She's convinced James and Barbara know more about Ashley's death then they've said.

Of course, Jared has not been charged with murder. But, come on, her torso was discovered under a tarp. Her arms and legs were found in a cardboard box. How could Ashley's death have been accidental?

And, court documents involving the perjury and accessory after the fact case against Jared's parents refer to the as a homicide investigation.

Kristine wants James and Barbara, as parents who must understand how she feels, to tell the police all they know.

"I just want my baby home. I just want, I want her home," Kristine Young says through her tears. "I need to know where my daughter is. I need to bring the rest of her home."

The staged TV event was Kristine's idea. She asked WOOD-TV to meet her outside the Chance's home.

"Barbara, as a mother, as a mother — your son is still breathing, and my daughter is not. You need to talk," Kristine begs.

"There are people out there that know something. Please, I need help finding her. I need help finding her, I do. I really do. I want her home," Kristine says. "I just want my baby.

"Ashley no longer has a voice, and I have to be. I have to be her voice."

Hours later, WOOD-TV scores an exclusive jailhouse interview with Jared. Reporter Heather Walker and her crew play the tape from earlier this evening when Kristine was standing on the front lawn of Chance's home in Holland Township.

Jared's on one side of a glass partition in the visitor's area. Heather Walker and her crew are on the other side. Jared and Heather communicate with a telephone handset.

He listens to Kristine's message over the phone.

Jared says he feels Kristine's pain and wishes there was something he could say to make her feel better.

"I want to give her some of that peace. I really would, um, but I don't. I don't even. I don't know what to do here. This situation is, I don't know what to do, so. I don't know what to say or do," Jared says.

But Jared stops short of saying he had anything to do with Ashley's death.

"What happened? I mean, you were friends with Ashley. She seemed like a lovely girl, a bright girl," WOOD-TV's Heather Walker asks Jared.

"She was, yeah," he answers.

Then Heather asks about what Jared discussed with his parents, what he might have told them about how Ashley died.

Jared stops. He freezes. He takes a deep breath and says, "I can't do this. I can't do this right now."

Jared slumps in his chair, takes a deep breath, exhales, and says,"I'm sorry, Ashley's mom. I apologize."

He hangs up the phone and then slowly walking back to his jail cell.

Interview over.

Chapter Eleven

Jan. 11, 2019

Kristine Young, on the witness stand, tells the Kent County judge faced with deciding whether Jared should stand trial for murder about texting her daughter, Ashley, Nov. 29, wondering why she hadn't heard from her.

Telling that part of the story is rough enough, but Kristine breaks down in tears as she identifies Ashley.

"How do you know, Ashley Young," Kristine is asked on the stand.

"She was my daughter," Kristine replies, forced to speak of her daughter in the past tense.

This is an emotional, crucial day for Kristine's family as well as Jared's.

Just yesterday, James Chance was bound over for trial on charges of perjury and being an accessory after the fact. Today, a Kent County judge will decide if Jared should face a murder charge in the death of Ashley Young.

Mario Nelson also testifies today in Kent County County Court, telling the story of how he and his girlfriend were so bothered by a foul odor coming from the basement of their home that he went downstairs, saw a stream of blood, and found the tarp covering Ashley's torso.

Dr. David Start takes the stand to say he believes Ashley died from trauma to her head or neck. Maybe she was strangled or smothered, Dr. Start says. Of course, it's hard to say without having Ashley's head. That's one of several body parts still missing. Start says he believes her body was cut up after she died.

Then, Jared's brother, Konrad, takes the stand, testifying that Jared pointed a revolver at him once, pulling the trigger several times. Holland Police records show a history of violence between the brothers that went beyond what is generally considered to be a normal sibling rivalry.

According to the police department's reports, drugs or alcohol were often involved in the brother v. brother conflicts.

Three years ago, Konrad and Jared got into a fistfight at the family home over bags of marijuana. Each brother claimed the other had stolen his supply of pot.

In February 2016, Konrad told police Jared had held a blowtorch to his face threatening to burn him and then hit him with a stick.

A month after that, the HPD was back at the Chance family home, responding to another report of the brothers fighting.

"Konrad is always able to run away from Jared because he is faster," their father told the police.

As Konrad leaves the courtroom today, he smiles at Jared, who nods in return.

Other than that, Jared shows not a flicker of emotion as he sits quietly at the defendant's table through it all, taking notes.

At the end of the day, the judge orders Jared to stand trial on a charge of open murder. That allows a jury to decide if he's guilty of premeditated or non-remediated murder. But in a way, it's just a question of semantics. Conviction on either charge would send Jared to prison for life.

You see, if convicted, Jared goes down as a four-time looser, a habitual offender. They throw the key away for people like that in Michigan.

So, no matter the charge, Jared's looking at spending the rest of his days behind bars if he's convicted.

But still, even as he's bound over for trial, Jared's not showing any emotion.

Chapter Twelve

Sept. 6, 2019

Jared's been a resident of the Kent County Jail for eight long months. It's one of the more pleasant facilities of its kind, but still, he's been living in a jail cell. At the same time, police and prosecutors have come up empty in their search for Ashley's head, hands, and feet. Not only would the missing body parts that Jared allegedly cut off and threw away like trash help pin down the cause of death, but their discovery would also allow Kristine Young to put her daughter, completely, to rest.

It's important to remember that push has come to shove in this case. Jared's trial on a charge of second-degree murder is set to start in three days, September 9.

So, prosecutors, today, come to Jared's attorney with a deal. They're willing to bypass Michigan's mandatory sentence of life in prison without any chance of parole if Jared will only tell them what happened to Ashley Young. Confess to the killing, tell police how and why the murder was committed, and of course, lead police to the rest of Ashley's remains. Those are the terms. A complete confession.

If Jared agrees to the deal, he would plead guilty to a charge of second-degree murder. In return, he would only face a minimum sentence of thirty-one-years in prison and a maximum sentence to be set by a Kent County judge.

Does that seem too lenient a punishment for a man who killed a woman, used a power saw to cut up her body to pieces, hiding the arms, and legs in a cardboard box and the torso under a tarp and the rest, who knows?

Well, it's okay with Kristine Young and her family. Kent County Prosecutor Chris Becker says the Young family signed off on the deal.

A hearing for the plea deal is expected to happen Monday morning, the same day that Jared's trial is set to begin.

Meanwhile, Jared's parents are still facing charges of felony perjury and being accessories to murder. There's no mention of them in this deal offer.

Chapter Thirteen

Sept. 9, 2019

Clean-shaven, wearing a blue oxford shirt that's open at the neck, Jared stands before Kent County Circuit Court Judge Mark Trusock to announce whether he'll accept a plea deal that would spare him a sentence of life in prison.

There aren't many in the courtroom who believe he's innocent or that Jared stands a chance of beating this case. So, his decision is, as far as they are concerned, a foregone conclusion.

But wait.

Perhaps, Jared is the only one who isn't convinced. Or maybe, he just doesn't want to have to lead the police to Ashley's remains that have yet to be found. Or could it be that he's innocent?

Whatever the reason, Jared knows another secret that nobody in court except, maybe, his lawyer shares. Jared's been thinking about this in a jail cell for the past three days. Jared's mind is made up.

Assistant Kent County Prosecutor Lawrence Boivin lays out the evidence the county has against Jared, the facts he is ready to present at trial.

Judge Trusock asks Jared if he's reached his decision. Will he accept the plea deal?

"I'd like to go to trial," Jared responds.

With that, Kristine's hopes that a plea deal would lead Jared to reveal how and why he'd killed Ashley, along with telling the GRPD what he'd done with the thirty-one-year-old woman's missing body parts are dashed.

Kristine might be crushed, but Judge Trusock tells Jared he doesn't care whether he accepts the guilty plea or chooses to go to trial. The decision is up to the defendant.

Now that Jared's told the court of his decision, the wheels of justice begin, again, to turn.

Jury selection starts only minutes after Jared announces his decision. Judge Trusock and the Kent County Court are ready. One-hundred prospective jurors who were waiting in another room are ushered into the courtroom.

Judge Trusock addresses the prospective jurors. He warns they are going to be confronted by five, graphic photos of body parts that will be difficult to look at. The judge tells the Kent County citizens in front of him, many of whom have never before even been inside the county courthouse in downtown Grand Rapids that nobody wants to see photos like these.

However, the jurors deciding this case will have to look at the photos. Judge Trusock asks if any have doubts about their ability to sit through a trial of this nature and see pictures so graphic.

One woman raises her hand. Judge Trusock excuses her.

The rest, ninety-nine people who could serve as Jared's peers, deciding if he's guilty of the gruesome murder of Ashley Young, remain.

Those selected to hear this trial will soon not only have to view the most gruesome photos they've ever seen; they'll be faced with a once-in-a-lifetime choice: should one of their fellow citizens spend the rest of his life in prison with no hope of freedom.

Chapter Fourteen

Sept. 13, 2019

Four days later, their work is finished. The men and women faced with the decision of sending Jared to prison for life return to the courtroom. They've reached a verdict.

During the trial, prosecutors said, even though the police never found her head, they believe Jared either shot the young woman in the head or bashed Ashley's head with enough force to kill her.

However, the county's deputy chief medical examiner also says on the stand that Ashley might have died of natural causes. But he adds that is highly unlikely.

However, her life did end abruptly. That much everyone can agree on. Once Ashley was dead, the prosecution contends, Jared decided to use a power saw to dismember the body in an attempt to hide his crime.

And, then, Kent County Assistant Prosecutor Lawrence Boivin says, Jared did nothing but lie to Kristine.

"How cruel is this man that he continues to lie to the mother of the person he's killed? He's giving her a carrot of hope that (Ashley's) alive," Boivin says in his closing argument this morning.

"But she's not. She's dead," Boivin adds. "And he's been mutilating her. And sawing her limbs off."

Jared's defense attorney, Andrew Rodenhouse, argues there was no evidence to convict his client. He says the GRPD botched the investigation, deciding prematurely that Jared was the killer.

"There were multiple other people who were potentially involved, but nobody bothered to take a DNA swab to at least exclude them," Rodenhouse tells jurors in his closing statements this morning.

Attorney Rodenhouse also questions why Jared would have wanted to kill Ashley.

"I've heard no motive and motive is not something that the prosecution has to prove, but for what purpose?" he says. "You saw the text messages. 'I just kissed him.' He admitted he liked her ... So did he intend to kill her? They have to prove that. I can't prove otherwise."

Kristine hasn't missed a day of the trial.

Every day, she sits in the courtroom, held by family and friends.

This day is no different.

Surrounded by her closest friends and family members, Kristine watches as the jury slowly files back into the courtroom to announce their decision. Will Jared spend the rest of his life in prison for killing Ashley Young?

Of course, he has no choice, but Jared is at the defendant's table today as he has been every day of the trial.

And today, just like every day of this trial, he's a rock. No emotion at all. Never a tremble. Never a frown or a smile. Nothing.

The jury began its deliberations at about 11:30 a.m. Now, at 3:10 p.m, they are back.

Three hours and forty minutes. It doesn't seem like much time to decide whether a young man, at the beginning of his adulthood, should wake up every day for the rest of his life in a prison cell. And it won't just be any prison cell. This man who's only had brief skirmishes with the law and only seen the inside of county jails will be sent to one of Michigan's maximum security state prisons.

A weighty decision. But the jury has heard enough.

The jury's verdict: Guilty of all charges; second-degree murder, concealing a death, three counts of tampering with evidence, and mutilation of a body.

So, pending appeals, Jared is going to prison for the rest of his life, with no hope of parole. He will never again be able to decide when he'll have breakfast, lunch, or dinner or what he'll eat at those meals. The only women he'll see are those wearing Michigan prison guard uniforms, and Jared will never shower alone.

It would seem that he's made his own hell.

Yet, as it stands now, Kristine is also trapped in, if not hell, then a kind of purgatory. She will spend the rest of her life always wondering what happened to her daughter, Ashley, how she was killed, and, more importantly, why she had to die.

Chapter Fifteen

Sept. 20, 2019

Jared Chance will spend the rest of his life behind bars. Kristine Young knows that, of course, but calls it "a hollow victory because my daughter is not here.

"Nothing will ease the pain of the family, friends, everyone's life she touched," Kristine says.

Now, Kristine says she needs more than Jared's guilty conviction. The woman who sat through every day of Jared's trial holding Ashley's cremated remains, wants the rest of her daughter to be returned to her.

When Jared refused the plea deal, which included a requirement that he reveal where Ashley's head, feet, and hands, are, Kristine was devastated.

She can't help but remember how open Ashley was to life and love. Yeah, that could make her gullible. Kristine remembers the time some friends told Ashley she'd need to go to an auto parts store to get blinker fluid for her car to make sure the turn signals worked.

Finally, someone told her it was a prank. Ashley just laughed it off.

As far as Kristine is concerned there never was anyone like her daughter, and she never again will meet anyone as special as Ashley.

Kristine is hurting. Bad. She needs to find the rest of her daughter to heal.

So Kristine and Ashley's stepmom, Dana Nelson, tell local reporters they are going to hold a motorcycle poker run to raise money to start a reward fund.

"I'm hoping someone will tell us where Ashley is," says Kristine.

With tears in her eyes, Kristine also remembers the day she spent furiously texting and calling every friend of Ashley's she could.

The day she died, instead of lying dead in the basement of Jared's duplex, Ashley was supposed to be visiting a friend in the hospital, then meet with Kristine to sign a lease on an apartment.

In addition, Ashley hadn't shown up to work. It was apparent something was wrong.

Kristine will never forget that day. She vividly remembers her body going cold at 5:45 a.m. If it was more than just a shiver or the feeling of goose or chill bumps. Kristine's arms and legs went numb.

She was afraid to tell anyone at the time or maybe even admit it to herself. But that's the moment Kristine knew something had gone terribly wrong.

Maybe at that moment, Ashley was trying to protect her, Kristine says.

"Sometimes, I feel like...she didn't want me to find her."

Chapter Sixteen

Oct. 10, 2019

Jared is being sentenced, today. The sentence has to be life in prison without parole, right? What else could it be?

Kristine cries as she tells a reporter that she'd like to see Jared put to death for taking the life of her daughter, Ashley. She can't get that satisfaction in Michigan. This isn't Texas, after all. Michigan abolished capital punishment back in 1846.

However, Kent County Judge Mark Trusock wants to make sure Jared spends the rest of his life in the hell that is the state's prison system. He'll get creative to accomplish that goal. Judge Trusock decides Jared should spend 100-to-200-years behind bars.

If that seems excessive, you're correct. It is. Make no mistake. The judge is sending a message. Trusock says he's intentionally surpassing state guidelines for second-degree murder and the rest of the crimes of which Jared's been convicted.

The judge says he wants to be sure Jared won't enjoy a breath of freedom until he is 130-years-old.

It wasn't only the brutality of killing Ashley then sawing her body into pieces that bother Trusock. He says part of the reason for the stiff sentence is the way Jared lied to Kristine after killing Ashley, along with his complete lack of repentance.

"What you did and what I saw in photographs was reprehensible and heinous," Trusock says to Jared as he passes sentence.

Jared, now wearing a light, well-trimmed red beard that follows his jawline, stares at the judge. His eyes aren't dead. Jared doesn't lack emotion or feeling. Pure hate comes from those eyes. If looks could kill, Mark Trusock might be drawing his last breath. But Jared has no power now. Not in this courtroom.

Jared's silent glare doesn't bother Judge Trusock, who mentions he has presided over more than 200 homicide and murder trials.

But still...

"This is without question the worst case that I have ever been involved in," the judge says. "You seemed at times to derive pleasure from the testimony that was best described as gruesome."

Trusock says it's his responsibility to keep a person like Jared away from society.

"You, sir, in my mind, are a very evil individual. You are clearly a monster without any conscience whatsoever," Trusock says. "You are someone who is a danger...and should never be allowed free."

Ashley's stepmother, Dana, who is also Kristine's longtime partner, pleads with Jared to reveal what he did with Ashley's hands, head, and feet. Dana tearfully recalls trying to comfort Kristine.

"(I hope) no one has to hear the sound that I heard coming from Ashley's mom the day she first, the first time she saw and was able to be with her daughter after she was murdered. After she was murdered. She only had her daughter's torso and limbs," Dana says, sobbing. "There was nothing I could do to take it away...to fix it for her. "Nothing."

Finally, holding a container filled with Ashley's ashes, Kristine has one last chance to speak to the man who murdered her daughter.

It's a powerful moment. Kristine's eyes are locked on Jared's.

"When I was eighteen, I was told I would never have children by a doctor. I thank God he gave me the gift of Ashley, even though it was for a very short period of time," Kristine yells. "God gave me that gift. You had no right to take her from me! to take her from her family!"

Jared is given a chance to speak. He declines

Ashley's family and friends cheer as he is led out of court, to spend the next 100 years behind bars.

James and Barbara, meanwhile, are accused of perjury and being an accessory after the fact. They are waiting for their days in court.

Chapter Seventeen

January 24, 2020

Jared's parents won't be able to visit him in prison for quite a while. James and Barbara Chance are going to be doing time in their own cells.

Barbara, charged with perjury and being an accessory to Ashley's dismemberment after the fact, entered pleas of no contest to all of the charges.

She could have gone to prison for life if she'd been convicted of perjury. But Kent County prosecutors agreed to a plea deal under which Barbara will do no more than one year in the county jail.

James, on the other hand, decided to take his case to court.

Prosecutors said that James' failure to tell them the family, with Jared in the car, stopped at a Costco along the Grandville-Wyoming border in suburban Grand Rapids and near the apartments along Kalamazoo Avenue could have affected the gathering of evidence.

And, they argued, since James is a retired cop from Illinois, he should have known, after Jared confessed to him to killing Ashley, that some parts of her body were in that cardboard box his son brought along with him on the trip home to Holland.

James, however, told police last month that he never suspected any body parts were in the box because he didn't smell anything that he could associate with a dead body.

James also told police when he was first interviewed that he had a bad memory and would often mix-up dates and even confuse the names of his two sons.

Prosecutors urged jurors not to believe James. They argued in court that James was only evasive. But the jury didn't totally buy their case.

James was found guilty of being an accessory after the fact in the dismemberment of Ashley. However, the jury decided James was not guilty of one count of perjury and deadlocked on the second perjury charge.

Kent County Prosecutor Chris Becker says today he won't retry the case. Since the jury dismissed one perjury charge, Becker doesn't think he has a chance of winning a conviction on the second charge.

So James will probably do no more than six months in jail on the accessory-after-the-fact conviction.

But here's the real bombshell from James' trial, and if the convicted perjurer isn't lying, it means there's no hope that Ashley's friends and family will ever find the missing body parts — her head, hands, and feet.

James says Jared "indicated to me" that he'd dropped those body parts in garbage cans all over metro Grand Rapids.

If true, that means Ashley's head, hands, and feet, are long gone — either incinerated or rotting in a landfill somewhere in West Michigan.

Tragic as it is, barring some unforeseen development, this shocking true-crime case is closed.

But then again, maybe not. There is still one unanswered question that Ashley's friends and family desperately want to be answered.

Why?

Collection of Breaking Shocking True Crime Stories

Homicide in the Backseat

Michael T. Gaffney, 21, and a nineteen-year-old friend, Francis Victoria Garcia, slipped out of a party in Hackensack, New Jersey, to have sex in the backseat of a car.

Something went wrong. Michael took a picture of a naked, and unconscious Francis, put it on Snapchat, and captioned it with a plea to his friends, "Just f***ed this b***h. I don't know what to do."

Less than half-an-hour later, Francis was dead.

Michael told his friends that they were having sex. At some point, he put his hands around Francis' neck. Before Michael knew what was happening, he says Francis' lips were purple, and he could feel air coming out of her nose.

The medical examiner says Michael was drunk with a blood-alcohol content of .256.

Michael faces a charge of reckless manslaughter now. He had not entered a plea when this blog post was published.

State Superior Court Judge Margaret Foti said during Michael's court hearing why his first reaction was to take a picture of Francis.

"I do find it curious that when a woman's body goes lifeless, or still, he takes a naked picture and posts it to 30 people," Judge Foti said.

Francis' family has the answer. They say Michael is nothing but a coward.

Husband Arrested, Wife's Remains Discovered;

"The World's Worst Nightmare," Says Her Mom

Rotting body parts found in Pleasant Valley, California: El Dorado County Sheriff's Office deputies arrested a California man on an outstanding domestic violence warrant and discovered what they believe to be the remains of his dead wife.

Anthony Gumina, hands cuffed behind him, sat on a curb, Saturday, with his little pet dog beside him, as deputies combed through every inch of his home and property.

Investigators believe Anthony killed his wife and say the evidence against him is "overwhelming."

But, Anthony's cousin, Robert Shawaluk, says he's "100 percent positive" that Anthony's innocent.

"He did nothing wrong. He loved her. He loved his wife," said Robert.

Anthony's wife, Heather Gumina Waters, a beautiful, blonde, 33-year-old, disappeared July 15. That was the same day she was released from a hospital after being treated for a broken collarbone.

"To protect the integrity" of the investigation,:" El Dorado deputies haven't released any other information.

However, Heather's mother, Joanna Russel, told KTXL-TV that she feared the worst when her daughter's car was found abandoned by the side of a road last month in El Dorado County.

And now, Joanna deals with the reality that her daughter is dead.

"I'm going to grieve for a very long time," Joanna said. "It's like the world's worst nightmare. But I know that she's in heaven now."

Cheerleader's Murder

Aaron Trejo, a seventeen-year-old high school football player, now destined to spend most of the rest of his life in prison, admits murdering his cheerleader girlfriend.

After murdering Breana Rouhselang, also seventeen-years-old, Aaron tossed her lifeless body into a restaurant dumpster.

Oh. Wait. Aaron did more than slay his girlfriend. His rage also claimed the life of their unborn baby. That's right, Breana was six months pregnant when Aaron lost his temper and killed her and their child.

Why? What was the spark that lit the time bomb of his temper?

Aaron, who decided to plead guilty to charges of murder and killing a fetus, told a South Bend homicide cop he blew his top when she told him she was pregnant.

"I took action," Aaron told the police. "I took her life."

Aaron told the detective he was pissed because she waited so long to tell him about the pregnancy, it was too late, he believed, for her to get an abortion.

He'll have up to eighty years to think about this in prison. That's the maximum sentence Aaron could receive in January 2020.

Killed in the Bronx

Noelia Mateo had no idea, as she got into her car parked on Ellsworth Avenue, in front of her home in the Throgs Neck neighborhood of the Bronx, New York, that it would be the beginning of the end.

Her grandson and daughter didn't have a clue, either. Both stood across the street, waving goodbye.

It was early, dawn, just 7 a.m. October 3. Autumn, according to the calendar, arrived a couple of weeks ago. But neither Noelia nor her grandkids could tell it by the weather. The steamy blanket of a heatwave that settled over the East Coast the last week of September had yet to be lifted.

Still, it was a good day to be alive.

It would also be the fifty-eight-year-old woman's last day to be alive.

As she got into her car, Noelia heard the throaty roar of a six-cylinder internal combustion engine coming at her. Maybe she sensed it more than heard it, but whatever, she looked up with her key in the car door's lock to see a car coming at her like a heat-seeking missile.

The car slammed into her auto before careening into a white van, hitting hard enough to leave the parked vehicle looking like an accordion. Her vehicle shoved forward by the impact, Noelia lay on the ground, broken, bleeding, pinned underneath.

The man who'd picked his automobile as a weapon of choice wasn't finished. He could see Noelia was still alive.

So, he pushed himself out of his wrecked vehicle, waving a machete, running back toward Noelia.

Choosing yet another weapon to carry out his homicide, the man jumped behind the wheel of Noelia's car, grabbing her keys on the way.

He started the car and incredibly, to the horror of Noelia's granddaughter, grandson, and the neighbors who were watching from living room windows, the man dropped the car into reverse and ran over Noelia.

The car slammed into a vehicle parked behind Noelia's car.

Now, with Noelia's twisted body laying on the street finally free of the car, but unable to do anything but crawl on broken bones, the man put the machete to work.

Standing over the woman, with her grandchildren standing shocked on the sidewalk across the street watching all of this, he brought the machete down across her body. Once. Twice. Three times he swung the sharp blade with murderous intent.

That was enough. The Bronx killer ran. But he'd failed. Noelia, a woman known for her happy smile and long brown curly hair, wasn't dead yet.

Her last moments of life, Noelia, with her body and mind forcing her to survive, crawled, covered with blood, on her hands, knees, and finally stomach, from the sidewalk to a patch of grass on the curb.

That's where Noelia died.

Neighbors now ran to help. One grabbed Noelia's shoes and handbag from the middle of the street and brought them to the curb. Another came running with a blanket to cover her body. Both waited by Noelia's side as they heard sirens coming closer.

Everybody on Ellsworth Avenue thought the world of Noelia. Everyone except her estranged husband, Victor Mateo. He is the prime suspect in this murder.

As this is written, the NYPD continues to look for Victor and investigate the case.

The police said the day after Noelia's life ended, they didn't know why she was killed, or if the attack was premeditated.

But one neighbor who stayed inside his house calling 911 to report the assault, screaming into his phone, "Where's the ambulance? Where's the police?" told the NY Times that the man who killed Noelia, "knew exactly what he was doing."

Crucifix Cracks Mommy's Skull

Christian Lydia Martinez spent the day drinking with friends. The twenty-five-year-old Texas woman came home, got into a fight with her mom, and cracked the forty-five-year-old over the head with a heavy, wooden crucifix.

San Antonio police say Christian ripped the religious icon right off the wall and bashed her mother over the head with it.

Mom's going to be okay. She suffered a skull fracture. But doctors at a local hospital were able to treat her injury.

Christian won't be coming home again, at least not for a while.

She's charged with aggravated assault with a deadly weapon and held on a $30,000 bond.

I don't think mommy's going to be putting up her house as collateral to spring her daughter, do you?

Hooker, Serial Killer, Or Both

Andrea Zamperoni, the head chef of Cipriani Dolce in New York's Grand Central Terminal vanished after finishing his Saturday night shift at the upscale, chic restaurant, August 17, 2019.

Two days later, when he failed to show up for work, fellow employees filed a missing person report with the NYPD.

It didn't take long to find the thirty-three-year-old who was described by his boss as a "sweetheart" and a "family man."

The missing person report came in Monday, August 19. Two days later, cops discovered Andrea's body at the Kamway Lodge & Tavern in Elmhurst, Queens.

That's near LaGuardia Airport. It's the kind of hotel where you can get a double room for $89 a night.

And a hooker was arrested.

Angelina Barini is accused of shooting up the chef with a fentanyl cocktail that led to an overdose.

Wait. There's more.

A law enforcement source told the New York Post Zamperoni might be only one of as many as five men who have fallen victim to the call girl's wiles and drugs. The NYPD says she made a career of slipping her johns this fentanyl-laced cocktail, then robbed them when they blacked out.

But fentanyl isn't an easy thing to handle. Angelina might have gone too far with Zamperoni. The same thing might have happened to a few other guys who were only looking for a good time.

Angelina is under investigation in as many as three other deaths, according to the NY Post.

The investigations continue.

However, NYPD Chief of Detectives Dermot Shea says his team has reason to be suspicious of this lady of the night.

"What we do know is there's a history here with Angelina," says Dermot Shea.

Serial Killers Everywhere

Serial killers are everywhere and about 40 percent of the time they are getting away with murder. So says a shocking true crime story in The Atlantic.

Rene Chun looks at statistics showing the nation's murders by serial killers have fallen 85 percent in the past three decades. But Chun also finds disturbing evidence from Thomas Hargrove, the founder of the Murder Accountability Project, that shows "at least 2 percent of orders are committed by serial offenders."

Do the math: If Hargrove is correct, Chun says that means there are at least 2,100 people out there committing serial killings who have not been caught.

How do so many murderous maniacs get away with it?

True crime author Michael Arntfield tells Chun serial killers are getting better at fooling the cops by doing things like planting false evidence.

The former police detective also points to weak police pay that leads to sub-standard detectives getting gold and silver shields. Let's face it: half of the nation's police detectives graduated in the bottom half of their classes.

And then there is the factor of growing isolation in our nation. People don't talk to each other like they used to. Sometimes minding our own business is not such a good thing, the way Arntfield sees it.

One more factor: We are much more mobile than we used to be. There are very few restrictions on travel in America.

Even though we all worry about the government using GPS to track our every step through our smartphones, the geography of the vast expanse of the USA makes it nearly impossible for

That's why the FBI said in 2016 the "ideal profession for a serial killer may well be as a long-haul truck driver."

It follows that the people most at risk are prostitutes.

"The victims in these cases," the FBI said, "are primarily women who are living high-risk, transient lifestyles. They are frequently picked up at truck stops or service stations."

Be careful out there. Serial killers—perhaps a couple thousand of them—are walking our streets and even sitting down beside us every day.

~~~

You can never get enough Shocking True Crime? Don't worry.
You'll always find more Shocking True Crime Stories and books at
www.rodkackley.com.

Bibliography

Audra Gamble. "Police search Holland home connected to body mutilation suspect." Holland Sentinel, posted 6 Dec. 2018, updated 7 Dec. 2018.

John McNeil. "Grand Rapids Police confirm I.D. of victim in grisly murder." WKZO Radio, posted 7 December 2018.

John Tunison. "Woman's remains found in man's basement identified as missing Kalamazoo woman." MLive, posted 8 December 2018.

Brendan Buffa. "Missing Kalamazoo woman's body ID'd by DNA, family spokesperson recalls her smile." WWMT-TV, posted 9 December 2018.

John Hogan. "Holland couple charged after son discloses he cut woman's body 'into multiple pieces.'" WZZM-TV, posted 12 December 2018, updated 13 December 2018.

Heather Walker. "Dismemberment victim's mom: 'I want my baby home.'" WOOD-TV, posted 14 December 2018.

WOOD TV 8 Staff. "Apologetic mutilation suspect: 'I don't know what to do.'" WOOD-TV, posted 14 December 2018.

Audra Gamble. "Bloody saw in mutilation case found in Holland parents' home." Holland Sentinel, posted 3 January 2019.

Michael Martin. "Docs" Evidence of cover-up found at Jared Chance's parents home." WXMI-TV, posted 3 January 2019.

Ken Kolker. "Police reports: History of bizarre behavior at Chance home." WOOD-TV, posted 10 January 2019, updated 11 January 2019.

24 Hour News 8 Staff. "GR man charged with murder, mutilation ordered to trial." WOOD-TV posted 11 January 2019.

Craig McCarthy, Andrew Denney, Chris Perez. "Prostitute Angelina Barini arrested in death of Cipriani Dolci's Andrea Zamperoni." New York Post, posted 26 August 2019.

Fox 17 News Staff. "Prosecutors offer plea deal to suspect in murder, mutilation case." WXMI-TV, posted 6 September 2019.

Becky Vargo. "Justice for Ashley. Grand Haven mother prepares for murder trial in daughter's death." Grand Haven Tribune, posted 6 September 2019.

Associated Press. "Plea deal in west Michigan dismemberment case seeks remains." Detroit News, posted 8 September 2019.

Megan Sheets and Ruth Styles. "Husband of missing California mom-of-three Heather Gumina is charged with homicide..." Daily Mail, posted 8 September 2019.

John Agar. "Jared Chance rejects plea deal in woman's killing, mutilation." MLive, posted 9 September 2019.

Barton Deiters. "Testimony: Murder Victim's mom describes frantic search." WOOD-TV, posted 10 September 2019.

John Agar. "Bartender noted no trouble between Jared Chance, young woman he allegedly killed, dismembered." MLive, posted 11 September 2019

WWMT Staff. "Jared Chance trial: Lieutenant spoke with suspect before Ashley Young was found." WWMT-TV, posted 12 September 2019.

Carolyn Muskens. "DNA: Blood on saw at Chance House in Holland is murder victim's." Holland Sentinel, posted 12 September 2019.

John Agar. "Jared Chance convicted of murder in killing, dismemberment of Ashley Young." MLive, posted 13 September 2019.

Emma Nicolas. "Jared Chance found guilty in woman's 2018 murder and dismemberment." WZZM-TV, posted 13 September 2019.

Fox 17 News. "Jury finds Jared Chance guilty of murder, mutilation." WXMI-TV, posted 13 September 2019.

Jon Mills. ": Ashley Young's mother says she needs daughter's missing remains to heal." WZZM-TV, posted 20 September 2019.

Michael Gold and Nate Schweber. "Man Kills Estranged Wife With Car and Machete in the Bronx, Police Say." New York Times, posted 4 October 2019.

Carolyn Muskens. "Chance parents' trial adjourned until 2020." Holland Sentinel, posted 10 October 2019.

John Tunison. "Jared Chance sentenced to 100 years for killing, dismembering Ashley Young." MLive, posted 10 October 2019.

WOOD-TV staff. "Family cheers as Ashley Young's killer gets 100-200 years." WOOD-TV, posted 10 October 2019.

13 On Your Side Staff. "Jared Chance gets 100 to 200 years for 'reprehensible and heinous murder.'" WZZM-TV, posted 10 October 2019, updated 11 October 2019.

Dorian Geiger. "'You Threw Her Out Like Trash,' Mom Clutches Daughter's Ashes as She Confronts Man Who Dismembered Her." Oxygen Crime News, posted 14 October 2019.

Rene Chun. "Modern Life Has Made It Easier for Serial Killers to Thrive." The Atlantic, posted 15 October 2019.

Maritza Salazar. "Woman accused of attacking her mother with heavy, wooden crucifix." Fox-TV San Antonio. posted 28 October 2019.

Caroline Torie. "Mishawaka teenager pleads guilty to murder, feticide of pregnant 17-year-old girlfriend." WSTB-TV, posted 30 October 2019.

Cecilia Levine. "Maywood Man Sent Snapchat of Unconscious Woman Before Getting Help, Report Says." Hackensack Daily Voice, posted 15 November 2019.

Jeana Gondek. "Jared Chance's mother enters no contest plea." WKZO AM/FM, posted 6 January 2020.

Barton Deiters. "Transcript: Dad said killer left body parts in trash." WOOD-TV, posted 9 January 2020.

WOOD-TV Staff, "No 2nd perjury trial for convicted killer's dad." WOOD-TV, posted 24 January 2020.

Other sources:

timeanddate.com. "Grand Rapids Weather History November 2018."

wunderground "Grand Rapids Weather History December 2018."

WOODTV "Police Video: Arresting Jared Chance." posted on YouTube 27 February 2019.

#JusticeForAshley and Justice for Ashley Young Facebook pages.

Don't miss out!

Visit the website below and you can sign up to receive emails whenever Rod Kackley publishes a new book. There's no charge and no obligation.

https://books2read.com/r/B-A-BYRB-SNOCB

BOOKS 2 READ

Connecting independent readers to independent writers.

Did you love *#Justice For Ashley*? Then you should read *The Murder of Thora Chamberlain*[1] by Rod Kackley!

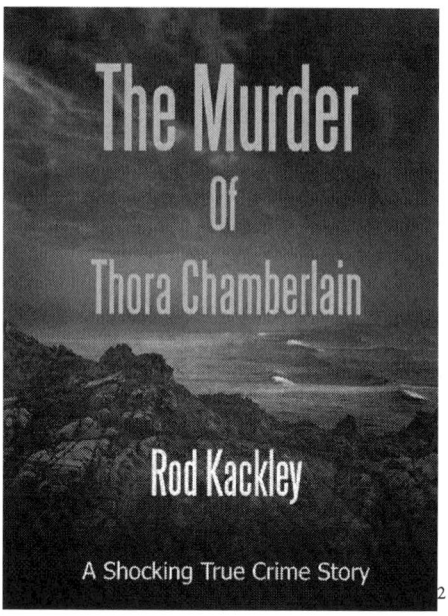

November 2, 1945: On her way to a high school football game with friends, a fourteen-year-old girl vanishes after driving away with a man who says he needs a babysitter.

The FBI unleashes its top kidnapping expert, an agent who helped bring John Dillinger down. Will that be enough to find the girl and her abductor?

Agents chase the suspected kidnapper from California to Illinois and back again.

---

1. https://books2read.com/u/m2YVOo

2. https://books2read.com/u/m2YVOo

Arrested in Los Angeles, he admits abducting the child. He also tells the FBI he killed the girl and threw her body into the Pacific Ocean. A search for her corpse proves fruitless.

Then, when all hope is lost, authorities discover the skeleton of another young woman who's fallen victim to this madman.

Ready for another twist? The wife of the man who made that discovery is found dead at the bottom of the cliff.

During the killer's trial, women around the country fall in love with the handsome monster and literally break down the doors of a courthouse to get close to him.

Wild enough for you?

Wait. We are just getting started.

After the child's killer is convicted and sentenced to the gas chamber, a scientist shows up and says he can bring the murderer back from the dead.

The Murder of Thora Chamberlain: A Shocking True Crime Story: This is the wildest, most shocking, true crime story you've ever read.

Also by Rod Kackley

Shocking True Crime Stories
Sleeping With The Devil: A Shocking True Crime Story of the
Most Evil Woman in Britain
Murder's Always Murder

Standalone
The Devil Made Him Do It: A Shocking True Crime Story of
Mass Murder
Mommy Deadliest: A Shocking True Crime Story of a Murder-
ing Mother
Sealed With A Kill: A Shocking True Crime Love Story
The Murder of Vanessa MacCormack
The Murder of Grace Millane

About the Author

Rod Kackley is an award-winning journalist and author, living and writing, in Grand Rapids, Michigan, USA.

Read more at www.rodkackley.com.

Printed in Great Britain
by Amazon

56032718R00043